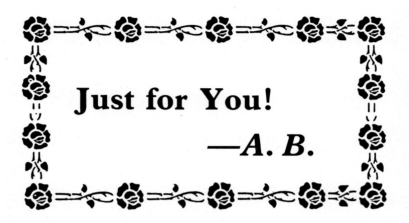

Just for You!
—*A. B.*

Endpaper photographs by
Harry V. Lacey

Frontispiece by
Paul Kwast

A Beginner's Guide to
Zebra Finches

Written by
Anmarie Barrie

Contents

1.
Pets

Whether you hang a small cage in the parlor, or build a garage-sized aviary in your yard, watching, caring for, and breeding Zebra Finches is an experience that will give you many hours of enjoyment. And of all domesti-

Fawn male Zebra Finch. Photo courtesy of Vogelpark Walsrode.

Recently imported African finches in a holding cage. Photo by Mervin F. Roberts.

cated birds, few are so beautiful and so diversified as this finch species.

There are literally hundreds of finch species. They are native to almost every corner of the globe; some species even being found quite close to the Arctic in Canada. As can be expected, however, they are most abundant in more moderate climates and in the tropics. They range in size from a little over a couple of inches to about fifteen or sixteen inches in length, counting the tail of such exotic species as the Paradise Whydahs. Almost every color, hue, and combination of colors is represented in their feathering. There is the strikingly beautiful Lady Gouldian Finch, almost a rainbow burst of shades of purple, yellow, red, blue and green. There are the solid color finches, such as the steel-blue Combassou and the Mannikins, mostly in shades of solid brown and black. I think if you were to view at one time just one of each finch existing today, it would put the rainbow itself to shame. In addition, many of the finches, although by no means all, have lovely songs. Yes, from Australia to South America, from India and Java to Mexico, you will find at least one kind of finch. The most popular of all finches is the Zebra Finch, but the information contained in this book applies to most of the following.

Australian Finches: Among the Australian finches the Lady Gould (*Poephila gouldiae gouldiae*) is the undisputed monarch. Experienced aviculturists and laymen alike rave until they run out of adjectives. Suffice it to say, the plumage of the Gouldians contains almost every color in the rainbow, in what seems an unbelievable arrangement. The Redheaded and Blackheaded Gouldians are the most beautiful; the Yellowheaded Gouldian the most rare. Fortunately, the Lady Gouldian is now being raised in the Orient as well as in the western Continent.

A female Red-headed Gouldian Finch. Photo by Michael Gilroy.

Fire finches, mannikins, and waxbills are suitable companions for Zebra Finches in a mixed collection. Photo by Harry V. Lacey.

The Spice Finch, or Nutmeg Mannikin, is one of the most popular finches. Photo by Klaus Paysan.

Of all the finches in captivity, these brightly plumed birds, with their clearly defined designs and patterns, are among the most beautiful. They are also excellent for breeding and easy to feed.

The Shafttail or Longtailed Grassfinch (*Poephila acuticauda acuticauda*) is a long, slender finch, exhibiting the typical Australian finch traits of striking contrasts. The head is gray, the beak bright orange. The feet are red. Bold black bars decorate its head and sides.

The glamorous Star Finch (*Poephila ruficauda*) is only a little less popular than the Lady Gould. It is a tiny little show-stopper with a red beak and head, an olive back, a rose-red tail. Its chest is bright yellow. Unlike many finches, the Star can carry a tune.

Like these Shafttails, most finches prefer a closed nest. Photo by A. Van den Nieuwenhiuzen.

In the wild, a Zebra Finch builds a nest that resembles this one. Photo by J. Wessels.

The Zebra Finch (*Poephila castanotis*) is a beginner's delight. Very inexpensive, easy to buy at almost any time of the year, quite attractive, it also multiplies like a computer. For starting breeders, the child-happy Zebra is exciting and rewarding. Identify it by its black and white barred chest, orange beak and legs. Also available in white, fawn, and mottled patterns, all of which have been obtained by breeding.

Parrot Finches: These are the finches with snob appeal. They are breathtakingly beautiful; but don't hold your breath waiting for one. They are also snobbishly rare and extremely expensive. Unfortunately, they have the high-strung temperament of many a rare beauty and they panic easily. The slighest noise may send these fast flyers hurtling into a painful collision with the flight wall.

The Pintailed Nonpareil (*Erythrura prasina*) is a calm ex-

It's easy to see why this finch is called the Cutthroat. The female lacks the red "ribbon" of the male. Photo by Paul Kwast.

ception, but it has its own eccentricities. Considered throughout Southeast Asia as a rice paddy robber, it is reluctant to eat anything else. If you want to change its eating habits you must resign yourself to a slow weaning process.

By mixing millet in with unhulled rice, it takes only a short period of time until the Nonpareil makes the transference. Not that unhulled rice is hard to obtain. Most large pet shops either have or can get it for you. However, it is easier if you can feed the same diet to all your birds.

Its beautiful colors, second only to those of the Lady Gould, and its availability during certain seasons certainly make it well worth considering.

Mannikins: Imported from India, Ceylon, Australia, Africa and the Philippines, the *Lonchura* species are popular in the United States. Less flamboyant in coloring than many finches, they provide a solid, striking contrast in an aviary. They are also inexpensive.

The Cutthroat or Ribbon Finch (*Amadina fasciata*) is a show-off. Rather large, occasionally aggressive, he must be given a wide berth while he sings and dances. The Cutthroat is named, not for any bloodthirsty habits, but for the bright red streak across his gullet.

The Society Finch or Bengalee (*Munia domestica*) is a popular cage bird. It is a fine breeder, and a reliable baby sitter for rarer breeds of finches who don't like to stay at home on their eggs. It too comes in a variety of colors including brown, fawn, white and mottled.

Waxbills: Most of the neat little Waxbills hail from Af-

Because of its strong parental instincts, the Society Finch is often used to rear the young of other finch species. Photo by Mervin F. Roberts

The Owl, or Bicheno, Finch, also native to Australia, is one of the closest relatives of the Zebra Finch. Photo by Pam Gardner.

Orange Cheek Waxbills are abundant in the wild and therefore frequently available in shops.

rica and are precise, fidgety little finches. Their beauty in most cases is in their precise patterns and unusual markings, rather than their bright colors. Most Waxbills are easy to obtain, but members of this large and diversified family range from the very common, like the Red Ear and Orange Cheek Waxbills, to the Lavender Waxbill, a rare and much sought-after beauty.

The Indian Strawberry (*Amandava amandava amandava*) is popular for its lovely song and equable disposition. It is a hardy finch that gets along well in an aviary or a cage. Like many other birds, the plumage of the Strawberry varies seasonally. In full mating plumage the male has a deep, almost black, back with a rich rust-colored head, neck and chest, sprinkled with small white spots. Out of color he resembles the female with all colors faded. The Strawberry male has a pretty little song.

18

Whydahs: The Paradise Whydah (*Steganura paradisaea*) is a flamboyant and magnificent bird. At maturity the male sports a fourteen-inch tail on his three-inch coal-black back. The chest is russet. Despite his impressive appearance, which never fails to win a fair hen, he is a mild-mannered bird. The male Paradise, like many other Whydahs, undergoes plumage eclipse after the breeding season. When he goes out of color he loses his long tail and deep coloration and he looks very much like the plain little lady he has just wooed. Poor girl, she is always a plain Jane, in color and shape resembling nothing so much as a common street sparrow. However, he loves her and that's what counts.

Whydahs are often called Widow Birds because of their black plumage and long tails which resemble mourning costumes. Far from mourning, though, the males use their tails for flirting. Many Whydahs are parasites,

The male Indian Strawberry loses his bright colors for part of the year. Photo by Michael Gilroy.

abandoning their eggs in other birds' nests.

Buntings: Yes, these are finches native to America. But federal law prohibits American bird owners from keeping native wild birds in captivity.

Warbling Finches and Seedeaters: The genus *Poospiza* is different from others in many respects. First of all, these South American Finches eat live food and fruit, as well as seeds. They are larger and more aggressive than the Australian or Waxbill finches. And their song is truly beautiful. Actually, these songbirds are a recent addition to the finch family. The British bred the first Warbling Finch in 1937, and even today this unusual bird is occasionally cultivated in Britain and the United States.

Cardinals: These large birds dominate smaller birds, but are still a welcome addition to any aviary. Of course, those found in the United States and Mexico cannot be legally kept here, but the bright, thin-beaked Cardinals from South America can be purchased easily and inexpensively. The Cardinal bridges the gap between hardbills and softbills because it eats almost anything.

2.
Selecting

Most naturally, you'll want a lovely, free-flying and brightly plumed Zebra Finch that's as healthy and fresh as all outdoors. There is no reason why a finch can't be in the best of health when you buy him. Surely, he

On Pied Zebras, like this hen, the normal markings are broken by patches of white. Photo courtesy of Vogelpark Walsrode.

When purchasing pets, make your choice from a group of sleek and alert Zebras like these, all in fine feather.

should be chipper and active, constantly hopping and flying from one perch to another; sleek, glossy and tight-feathered.

Got your bird? Then look around for a companion. He'll stay more cheerful and healthy if he has a friend around.

In many varieties of finches, the male acquires a fuller, more magnificent plumage at mating time. Some finches, like the Strawberry, merely become more intense, more glossy in color. Others, such as the Weaver and Whydah, turn into completely different birds. When a bird is "in color" his personality often changes, and he becomes more proud and aggressive. At other times, about four to six months of the year, he resembles the inconspicuous female. Zebra Finch males are more colorful than females, except for whites.

Whatever kind of finch you buy, the home you select for him should be large and roomy. The size of the bird will determine the size of the cage, but be very careful to get a cage with narrow spaces between the bars for the Zebras and other small finches. Most finches are so much slimmer than softbills that they can slip through the bars of ordinary cages. **Ask your pet shop owner for help;** he will suggest a wide variety of possible sizes and types of cages. We recommend a durable chrome, stainless steel or electroplated finish, rather than a painted finish. The former won't rust, shatter or peel. And for a reasonable investment you'll have a beautiful and lasting showplace for your bird.

If you have only one or two finches, a standard canary cage is most satisfactory if the bars are close-set. If you want several pairs of finches, you'll be pleased to know

When Zebras are mature, as these two are, it's easy to distinguish females from males. Photo by Mervin F. Roberts.

you don't have to build an aviary in the back yard. A standard flight cage is very comfortable for your birds, and easy for you to stock and clean. Some large flight cages come on casters so you can move them from living room to patio or wherever you wish.

You can arrange the swings and perches yourself. Especially in a large flight, it is important that the perches and swings be staggered so all the birds have freedom to fly and hop, with a variety of routes from which to choose. Take care not to put one perch above another or the droppings will fall on the lower level birds.

Moving up to an aviary

For those lucky enough to have a yard, an aviary is a fun project; fun to plan, fun to build, and fun to observe. The only fundamentals are a covered shelter and a large flying area. In temperate climates the shelter and flight can be continuous; in colder areas the shelter should have its own closing door. The size will depend on the number of finches you house and how well they get along. If you intend to breed your finches, divide your aviary into several flights. Some finches are compatible, but some are veritable hermits; some are aggressive, some shy. And in the clash of personalities, breeding suffers.

Almost any garden setting is ideal for an aviary, as long as it is out of the wind's path. Build your aviary with an eye for beauty. Don't make the mistake of housing your birds in a place that looks like a chicken roost. After all, you bought your finches for beauty and pleasure, but breeding Zebra Finches can be very profitable too.

Most mutations in Zebra Finches have resulted in a dilution of the normal colors, as this male shows. Photo by Paul Kwast.

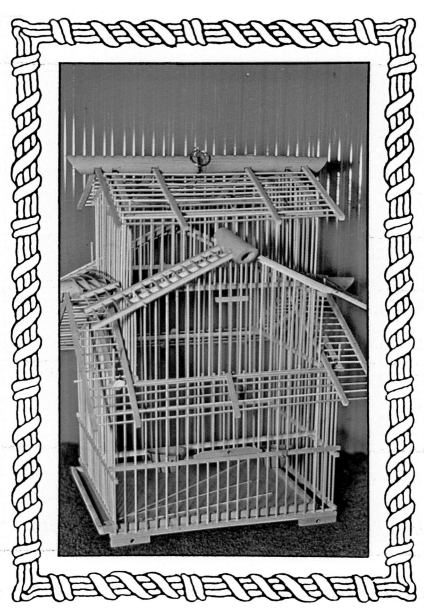

A bamboo cage of this sort is suited only to a single pair of finches. Photo by Dr. M. Vriends.

3.
Housing

There are many lush and sturdy plants you can buy for your aviary. They not only brighten up the flight, they also provide many new and unusual perches for your birds. They even attract insects, an extra treat in your

In Zebra Finches, the crest mutation ordinarily produces untidy results. Photo by Vogelpark Walsrode.

The tail of the normal Zebra Finch is boldly marked with black and white. Photo by Michael Gilroy.

bird's diet. Ask your nurseryman which trees, bushes or plants thrive best in your climate.

Furnish your aviary carefully. It should have all the necessary equipment, but not so much that it becomes a cluttered eyesore.

Ideally, you'll need enough feeders for a five course meal: at least one each for seeds, water, health grit, insect food mix, and dietary supplement; and a separate bath dish. You wouldn't bathe in a water glass after dinner. Don't force your Zebra Finch into bad table manners either.

Perches should be of varying thicknesses so that all sizes and shapes of birds can grip the bars easily. A bad perch can cause trouble to birds with long toenails. Finches scrape their beaks on the perches, so keep them clean at all times. We recommend wooden dowels, since they are so easy to clean, but these should be supplemented with branches for variety.

If you live in a cold climate, be sure your aviary is heated thermostatically. Electric heaters which give off a mild heat are recommended, rather than oil or gas heaters, which have an unpleasant odor and may asphyxiate the birds.

In any climate, a night light is essential. This need be nothing more than a small-size bulb near the feeders. When a finch is ill, the warmth of an electric bulb might be all that is required to sustain him until nature brings him back to health. Food should be placed on the floor if he rests there instead of on his usual perch.

Optional furnishings you may want to buy are nests and nesting hair, available at pet shops, and small bits of cloth or gauze, all of which are used by the birds when breeding. Other decorative items are gourds, palm leaves, dried grass, etc.

A bank of wire-mesh cages used for breeding finches. Each cage houses one pair. Photo by Terry Dunham.

4.
Feeding

Zebra Finches are designated as hardbills because their basic diet is seed. For breeding birds, or even for those you purchase just for their beauty, you should plan a varied diet. In addition to mixes of millet and canary

A pied female Zebra Finch. Photo courtesy of Vogelpark Walsrode.

seeds, available at pet shops, your finch should eat gravel or grit, greens, a finch treat food, and cuttlebone. Many finches prefer their basic millet seed in the natural form as it is grown in sprays or sprigs. Finches also enjoy dehydrated fruits and vegetables, including greens, which can be bought at most pet shops.

A good basic mixture for Zebra Finches consists of equal parts of large white millet, red millet and german finch millet. Small amounts of specialty seeds such as hemp, canary, thistle, flax, sesame or oats may be added to the mix or offered separately. Some of the larger finches also appreciate unhulled or paddy rice. It is also advisable to add a few mealworms to a mixed collection two or three times a week. If these are not available a packaged Mynah Bird meal, moistened with water, may be substituted in a separate dish.

For cages housing one or two birds, the usual food and water cups, plus a treat cup, are all that is required. For aviaries housing a larger assortment, the different foods are kept in separate feeders so you can more easily determine which food needs replenishment.

5.
Health

Luckily, Zebra Finches are staunch little birds and don't contract diseases readily, but there are several signs to watch for. If his eyes get dull, his feathers drab and puffy, and he is lethargic and slow, your bird is

In the variety called Cream, the coloration has become very subtle. Photo courtesy of Vogelpark Walsrode.

Greens are appealing to Zebra Finches. Because of the vitamin content, such dietary items help to maintain health. Photo by Mervin F. Roberts.

probably ill. Be alert for loss of weight. Place a wide variety of tempting foods within easy reach, close to perches, or on the floor if the bird is not roosting.

Heat also helps. Try to maintain a temperature of 80 to 90F. in the cage. The light bulb previously mentioned will help to retain the heat and so will a cage cover. A constant temperature must be maintained night and day. Don't worry about the light's keeping your bird awake. He'll just tuck his head under his wing and doze right off.

Treating ailments and accidents: Occasionally these extremely fast flying birds suffer a broken leg or wing. Fortunately, treatment is fairly easy and we present it to you as recommended by L.E. Fisher, D.V.M., Director, Lincoln Park Zoo.

For fracture repair of broken leg: Stretch the leg straight from the body by holding the toes with gentle traction outward. Then using one-half inch adhesive tape, place it behind the areas of the break and then in front, letting the edges stick together. Make several turns of the tape around the leg, then trim away any excess tape, leaving about an eighth inch at each side of the leg. Leave on for approximately ten days. If the break is in the thigh area, high up on the leg next to the body, pull the leg up in a sitting leg position and tape it to the body for approximately ten days.

For fracture repair of broken wings: Place the involved wing in its natural position next to the body. Then take a short strip of one-quarter inch adhesive tape and tape the wing ends together at the back of the body. After the wings are fixed, take a strip of tape around the wings and body, encompassing all. Leave

The principal food of Zebra Finches is a mixture of small seeds. Photo by Mervin F. Roberts.

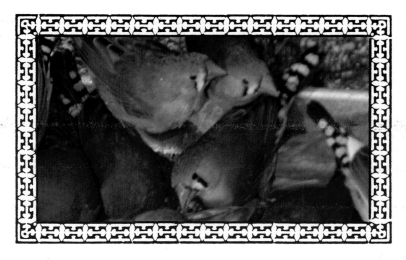

The Zebra Finch no doubt receives its name from the throat markings of the wild-colored male. Photo by Paul Kwast.

These varieties, from top to bottom, are Penguin, Fawn, and Silver. Drawing by R. A. Vowles.

Mashed hard-boiled egg is probably the most significant dietary supplement for Zebra Finches. Photo by Mervin F. Roberts.

the tape on for approximately ten days.

While treating birds with broken legs or wings, it is a good idea to remove the perches from the cage. Also, food and water in shallow cups should be placed on the cage floor in case a bird with a broken leg or wing cannot get up to a perch to reach it.

To facilitate tape removal from the legs or wings, use acetone, if available, or any tape-dissolving liquid.

Colds: Symptoms: Looks puffed up, listless. Bird shivers and occasionally sneezes. An early symptom is a slight watery discharge from the nose. Droppings white and watery.

Treatment: If he stays on the bottom of the cage quite a bit, food and water cups should be placed close to him. Some of the softer supplementary foods like condition or egg biscuit should be moistened with a commercially prepared liquid tonic available at most pet shops

Heat, as mentioned previously, is important. Speak to your veterinarian about antibiotics.

Constipation: Symptoms: Infrequent and hard droppings. Bird appears unable to evacuate without jerky movement and apparent discomfort. General listlessness.

Treatment: Add more greens to the diet. If constipation is severe, give your bird one drop of mineral oil with a medicine dropper. Allow more exercise.

Diarrhea: Symptoms: Loose droppings with unusually large amount of white matter. Vent feathers slightly wet at first, then more and more soiled. The bird will be in-

Feather lice on the underside of a bird's wing. Photo by Manfred Heidenreich.

A pair of Zebras in a wicker nest. Photo by Harry V. Lacey.

Preening is important to cleanliness and to health. In Zebra pairs, males and females preen one another. Photo by Harry V. Lacey.

active and sit with ruffled feathers.

Treatment: Withhold green foods for a few days, feeding entirely on seed. Some experts recommend fresh buttermilk instead of drinking water during intestinal troubles.

Asthma: Asthma may be caused by drafts and bad ventilation of breeding rooms. The most common cause is a dirty cage that permits the birds to breathe dust, which inflames the respiratory organs.

Symptoms: Breathes laboriously, gasping for air. Each breath may be accompanied by wheezing or squeaking.

Treatment: The same as for colds.

Overgrown claws may result from inadequate flying space and improper perches. Photo by Leslie Arnall.

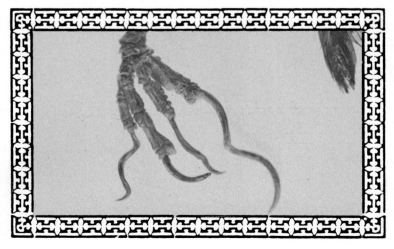

A newly hatched Zebra chick is covered with sparse down. Photo by Mervin F. Roberts.

Baldness: Sometimes baldness may be caused by mites. First, if you find mites, follow the treatment listed for them. If the cage is placed too near a radiator or stove, this could also cause excessive shedding and baldness. Remove at once to a more moderate temperature. The addition of a bird multi-vitamin to the diet is indicated.

Sore eyes: Symptoms: Your pet may start rubbing the sides of his head against his perch or against his cage. Eyelids and eyes become inflamed and reddish.

Treatment: Wash your pet's eyes with a mild boric acid solution. Add a drop or two of cod-liver oil to his seed cup daily to counter vitamin A deficiency.

Sore feet: If you care for your pet properly he is unlikely to get sore feet. The main cause is a dirty cage. Other causes are rough perches. Prevention is the an-

Zebra Finches are active enough by nature to profit from spacious accommodations. Photo by Harry V. Lacey.

A female of one of the more uncommon varieties: Penguin, which is charac-terized by white from the chin to the belly. Photo by Paul Kwast.

swer here. Provide good care, and treatment will not be needed.

Treatment: Wash your pet's feet in warm water. Dry thoroughly. A light coating of petrolatum may be applied daily.

External parasites: All birds, wild birds as well as cage birds, may be bothered by mites and lice.

Treatment: Treatment of mites involves two stages. You must kill the parasites on the birds and at the same time exterminate all the mites in the cage. If you find mites on your finch, remove him from his cage and apply one of the many good powders that are available. Apply it directly to the bird's body, especially under the wings. Work it well into the feathers. Aerosol sprays are also available and may be easier to use as you need not remove the bird from the cage. Mites may be exterminated from the cage by one of several methods. Use one of the mite powders. Apply kerosene with a small brush to all places where they may lurk. Clean the cage with boiling water and then use a good disinfectant. Make sure the cage is thoroughly dry before returning the bird to his home. Replace all perches with new ones.

Signs of parasites are holes in the bird's feathers, frequent scratching, drops of blood on the perch, restlessness at night, and of course actual sight of the parasite, either on the bird itself or in the cracks of the cage.

6.
Breeding

Most finches are social and will breed. Whether you have an aviary full of finches, or just one caged couple, you can find enjoyment in breeding your birds. All you have to do is encourage them to lay their eggs.

In this variety, the male's cheek patches have lost their color. Photo courtesy of Vogelpark Walsrode.

If you are a beginner, you should start with Zebra Finches.

Zebra Finches lay their eggs in nests, so the first step is to provide a nesting place. You can get nesting material, including the finch nests, at your pet shop. Most birds prefer a closed nest—a box or hollowed-out tree branch—with about a one inch opening. A dried gourd with a hole cut in the side makes an ornamental and practical nest. Be sure to provide perches on this type of nest. Experiment a little to determine where to put the nest. Some birds like it high, some like it low. Keep changing the position of the nest until your finch settles happily in it.

It is not unusual for Zebra hens to lay a clutch of as many eggs as this. Photo by Ray Hanson.

On these Zebra nestlings, many feathers are still in their sheaths. Photo by Mervin F. Roberts.

Sometimes a condition called eggbinding will occur. The female will not be able to drop the egg and will use up all her energy trying. If your bird seems listless, and you see a puffiness above the vent, insert olive or baby

Since Zebra chicks hatch almost naked, they must be brooded by their parents. Photo by Mervin F. Roberts.

oil with an eyedropper into the vent to ease the passage. You must catch this disorder early, before the strain saps the bird's strength completely and she dies. If she fails to pass the egg in twenty-four hours after the application, try to assist by inserting the eyedropper to break the egg. This is a drastic method to be used after all other remedies have failed.

Depending on the temperature of the nest, it takes about two weeks after the eggs are laid before they hatch. The number of eggs varies depending on the species and the individual parents. In most species, both mother and father sit on the eggs. In fact, the male often seems much more interested than the female. Often a nest of eggs has been hatched long after the mother has "flown the coop".

7.
Training

You'll enjoy your Zebra most by just watching and admiring him. He may sing, but not on cue. He may swing, but only as the swinging spirit moves him. Don't

A Penguin hen seen from behind. Photo courtesy of Vogelpark Walsrode.

expect to train these free-winging little creatures too much.

In many instances, finches can be sufficiently tamed to sit on your finger or eat from your hand. Slowly allow him to become accustomed to your presence by the cage. Speak softly and gently. Then put a bit of bird seed on your forefinger and put your hand in the cage, tempting him to come. Hold very still. At first, perhaps, he'll be too shy to hop right on. Don't frighten him, just encourage him. Before you know it, he'll be looking forward to your visits and he'll just hop right on your finger, anticipating a bit of seed or green! Be patient in your training and you'll be well rewarded.

When you realize the many varieties of finches, their diverse habits, characteristics and personalities, it is easy to see why beginning bird fanciers soon become dedi-

Since Zebra Finches are domesticated, they are steady toward people, though not naturally tame. Photo by Harry V. Lacey.

A Zebra chick just old enough to have left the nest. Photo by Mervin F. Roberts.

cated aviculturists. Only with finches can you capture in your own home all the excitement, busy-ness and beauty of woods, forests and jungles all over the world.

Although we have been able only to skim the surface of finch raising, you can see that there is much more to a bird than a cute little singer on a swing. Finches are beautiful to look at, challenging to acclimate and breed, fun to watch and admire.

We know of one little girl who was a shut-in for several weeks. Her parents set a cage in her room and moved in two Zebra Finches to keep her company. When the girl had returned to school her teacher would often see her staring off into space, sometimes ignoring the other children. When asked if she was sorry to be back in school, she replied, "Oh, no, but I miss my birds". She echoes the feelings of many who have come to under-

In many respects, tree branches are the best perches for finches. The varying thickness exercises the feet. Photo by Paul Kwast.

A pair of Penguin Zebras perched atop their nest. Photo by Harry V. Lacey.

stand, appreciate and love our winged friends.

Because the Zebra Finch is available in so many different color varieties it is extremely popular. Many bird lovers, however, claim the converse. They claim that because the bird is so popular many people have bred them, and the result is the proliferation plus the proliferation of different mutants. What this all means to you, the Zebra Finch owner, is that there are more color varieties of Zebra Finches available than any other finch. The Zebra Finches are available in the following color patterns:

• White Zebra Finch. Both males and females have almost a snow-white feather coloration, but they still show their beautiful red beak. It is difficult to distinguish sex in the white color variety.

• Chestnut-flanked White. The males are white but keep the very faint images of the cheek patch, chest bars, and the marks on its flank. The hens, on the other hand, are white except for the black mark at the eye, and a very light fawn belly region.

• Fawn. The grays and blacks of the normal wild variety are replaced by a brown and a diminished brown which is tan. This is true for both males and females.

• Dilute. These Zebra Finches have all of their colors faded. If you take the normal markings on a normal Zebra Finch, and consider them lightened, then you have a silver. Fawns are lightened to very light tan colored specimens.

• Penguin. The males have a chest-bar area and orange cheek patches that are replaced by silvery-white plumage.

Depicted here are a Chestnut-flanked White pair above and a Fawn pair below.

The Florida Fancy is one of the newest Zebra mutations. Photo by Dan Martin.

The difference in coloration between the normal gray and the Fawn is apparent here. Photo by Paul Kwast.

• Pied. Pigment disappears from some areas of the plumage, which are therefore white. The most handsome Pieds are those in which the markings are symmetrical. Some breeders have developed strains called Saddle-pieds in which the only remaining pigment is on the back between the wings.

• Florida Fancy. The handsomest of all the Zebra Finch mutations, the Florida Fancy—or whatever the international, British-based Zebra Finch Society ultimately calls it—is the most recent of the Zebra mutations, having appeared in the late seventies in the Florida aviaries of breeder Hazel Kipp. It is white, like the Chestnut-flanked White, but the chest bars, flank markings, and cheek patches of the male appear in the vivid colors of the Normal variety, making it a striking bird.

Other color varieties include the Black-breasted Zebra Finch, in which the black breast bars form a solid black mass, and the Yellow-beaked variety. These are rare in the U.S. at present, but will become more common with time.

Two other varieties are not color mutations but rather mutations in the arrangement of the feathers themselves, whatever the color of the bird in question. Frills have feathers curving out from the body, resulting in an appearance most commonly described as being like a feather duster. The description is far more common than the bird is. The second mutation of feather arrangement produces a crested bird, with feathers lying on the crown of the head like a Beatle haircut. Crested Zebra Finches generally are worth three to five times as much as noncrested Zebras.

Suggested Reading

HANDBOOK OF ZEBRA FINCHES
By Dr. Matthew M. Vriends
ISBN 0-87666-886-4
TFH H-1020

Contents: The Zebra Finch and Its Care. Tips for the Bird Enthusiast. Historical Background. Breeding in a Colony, Breeding Cage or Aviary. The Breeding Season. Brooding. Curious Behavior Patterns During Brooding. Champion Birds Through Painstaking Selection. Special Attention for Young Zebra Finches. Which Nesting Boxes Do Zebra Finches Use? Perches and Sleeping Places. Food and Drinking Water. Proper Management. Sickness and Accidents. Heredity and Crossing. How did the Breeding of Zebra Finches Develop? Introduction to Heredity. Crossings. New Breeding Possibilities. Other Small Exotic Birds.

Audience: For everyone—beginning bird fanciers, long-experienced aviculturists, even professional breeders—interested in the most popular pet finch species. Highly illustrated with both color and black and white photos of the many different color variations, this book is especially valuable for breeders who want to learn about the genetics of zebra finches.
Hard cover, 256 pages, 5½ x 8
87 full-color photos, 138 black and white photos, 16 line drawings.

FINCHES AND SOFT-BILLED BIRDS
By Henry Bates and Robert Busenbark
ISBN 0-87666-421-4
TFH H-908

Audience: The most complete book on seed-eating, soft-billed birds (as opposed to "hard-billed" or parrot-like birds). Every important cage bird is discussed and illustrated in color. No other book in any language has so many birds known in the pet bird world. Used extensively all over the world as an identification guide. A must for bird reference libraries for pet shops, zoos, general reference libraries and for governmental agencies concerned with the identification of birds. High school level.
Hard cover, 5½ x 8½", 735 pages
159 black and white photos, 246 color photos.

BREEDING BIRDS AT HOME
By Jurgen Nicolai
ISBN 0-87666-841-4
TFH H-1038

Contents: Breeding in Aviaries. Grass Finches and Waxbills. Whydahs. Finches. Thrushes. Warblers and Flycatchers. Doves. Index.

Audience: This book provides a general discussion of bird husbandry and the breeding cycle from start to finish. Included are many practical suggestions about nesting material, preferences of certain groups of birds, and relations between parents and young. High school level.
Hard cover, 5½ x 8", 160 pages
141 full-color photos, 28 black and white photos.